Ghost Stories

Paul Kuipa

Published by Paul Kuipa, 2022.

GHOST STORIES

First edition. April 11, 2022.

ISBN: 979-8201253448

Written by Paul Kuipa.

Also by Paul Kuipa

Testimony Of The Resurrected
In Love With A Siren
The Walk Of Faith
Amelia The Young Witch
The Life Of A Prophet
Ghost Stories

FORWARD

A **ghost** is the soul or spirit of a dead person or animal that can appear to the living. In ghost lore, descriptions of ghosts vary widely from an invisible presence to translucent or barely visible wispy shapes, to realistic, lifelike forms.

Have you ever felt a sudden cold chill or seen something move out of the corner of your eye? There are those who believe that these kinds of occurrences are explainable and believe that they may be caused by ghosts or other paranormal activity. Ask a crowd of people and you are sure to find at least one person who's had a firsthand experience with the supernatural.

The word ghost and spirit interchangeably, but there is strong difference between them

Ghosts are similar to psychotic human beings, incapable of reasoning themselves. Spirits on the other hand are the surviving personalities of all of us who pass through the door of death in a relatively fashionable way. Ghosts are tied to the location of their death. In most cases they have unfinished business, as the deceased does not accept the way they died. Some don't know that they are dead.

The simplest form of unfinished business can be as innocent as a person being attached so strongly to their home that they cannot leave it behind and pass over. They are known as "caretakers" and want to stay to make sure the building is being taken care of properly by future owners, as well as to their approval. At the other end of the scale, unfinished business can take the form of dark energy when a person's death is extremely violent and unexpected.

Here are some real stories of ghost encounters stories so creepy that you may leave the lights on tonight.

Chapter One

The Man In Black

"The Man In Black", still haunts the living hell out of me.

I was 14 by that time and was very prayerful. I was tormented by weird looking shadows but at a point, they all disappeared. On this fateful day however, I was told to pray whenever I go to bed because of those shadows and weird dreams I have every night. I refused to pray and went to bed.

It was a bunk bed and I was sleeping on top while my sister was sleeping down. I couldn't dream at all so I decided to sleep facing the wall. Nothing happened for about 30 minutes but then I saw something strange in my dream. Remember, my eyes were only closed so it came as a shock when I saw something as if I was dreaming while being awake.

I saw a black figure very inhumanly tall. His face is as dark as the color black but to my dismay, he had no eyes or face, just a dark shape wearing a black hat. His nails were long and his toenails too. He wore a black suit and pants and tie.

Upon seeing this, I woke up in fear just to realize that I was paralyzed on my bed. I couldn't move a muscle and couldn't see what was going on behind me. Hopefully, I turned to face the wall earlier and still thank heavens for doing so. The temperature around me dropped and I felt an eerie presence. Suddenly, I felt two hands grabbing me by my shoulders trying to turn me around to face it.

I recognized the hands of that weird thing I saw minutes ago in my supposed dream because of the nails. I started crying but couldn't pray. It was like a force was holding me still and another one trying to turn me over. After some minutes of struggle, it finally let go of me and I fell from my bunk bed and knocked my head in the process. I passed out!

The next day I woke up normally in my bed as if none of the accidents from earlier happened. I went to the kitchen and met my dad doing his usual stuff.

I'm not taking illegal substances or hallucinating but why did everything sound normal? And why did I wake up in my bed? I touched my head to feel the agonizing pain. I asked my family if they saw me laying on the floor but they said no.

This mystery will forever haunt me and that thing or man will forever torment me.

My Friend's Haunted House

So this is a creepy story nine years ago fresh out of grad School came back home to help a friend clean out his parents' house. They we beaten and killed, mother was raped repeatedly throughout the night. We have been friends since we were seven years old. Neither one of us knew what happened. We were both in school at the time the Neighbors found them.

Her older sister identified them so when we went through the house giving clothes to goodwill, setting things aside to sell everything that was not on the will. He was an only child so it was all his giant TV, furniture and all the tools. Its amazing looking back not remembering seeing any blood or a struggle as far as we know no one besides the police. We were in the house and got tired after a while then fell asleep in the living room...At 3:00 are we're disturbed by loud bangs all around the house nonstop for over twenty minutes.

By this time we already had guns in our hands then abruptly stopped. We opened the front door searching for where the noise was the loudest with our guns drawn and of course nothing was there. I stayed a few more nights. He didn't want to be alone. We started arguing over nothing and we were at each other's throats ready to kill. I left him but he followed me yelling until us both ended up in the front yard and all the mood behavior was gone. As we regained ourselves trying to figure out what happened and why we were arguing to the extent of nearly killing each other. I just took a look at the second floor window and I saw a man standing there in all black just staring at us, giving an evil smile and grin and disappearing. From that day I never stepped foot in the house again, not even to get my wallet or keys I left. I just heard that he later had it demolished shortly after

New Year's Eve

On New Year's Eve my wife and I were sitting on our couch watching TV. It was about 10:30 at night. We have a deck that runs along the back of our house and there are two doors that open onto it. One from the kitchen and one from the dining room. From the couch we can see the door in the dining room and it is glass so we can see through it. We use the door in the kitchen as our main door to come in and out of the house. So we were sitting on the couch and there were three very loud knocks on the door in the kitchen. I got up to see who was there and before I got there, another three loud knocks were heard but this times it was louder than before. As if someone is impatient. My wife even commented on it as I was walking to the door.

I opened the door and no one was there. There was snow on the ground and there were no tracks in the snow. I walked off the deck into the driveway. I called out "Hello" and "Can I help you" but got no answer. I turned around to go back inside. I could see the door to the dining room. There were three more knocks on the glass on that door, but no one I could see was there. But as I was looking through it, it seemed like something invisible was knocking. I called out again, but still got no answer.

My wife was looking at the glass door when the knocks happened and she saw no one either.

Two Whispers

Macy lived on a typical prairie farm; a creek ran through the farm so that was great fun in the summer....

Macy was born into a large family and she was the youngest, all of her siblings were much older so she didn't have anyone to hang around with till one summer when she met a boy about her age down by the creek...

Glenn loved going to the farm at Short Point creek, the farm was pretty typical, Glenn's distant relatives owned the land but he had been told a few times that this farm had originally been owned by his third great grandpa...

The farm did have two features that interested Glenn immensely...

One was a short point creek, the other was the old school house that was close to the creek, it was on the family land but he had been told by his relatives to never enter the old school because it was very old and could fall down anytime...

Glenn didn't believe the school was going to fall down, in fact despite the fact that it had not been used in decades it looked very solid...

Glenn never went in there because it looked very spooky, even during the day... On one visit to the farm Glenn met a girl about his own age down by the creek, Glenn was 10 and his interest in girls had recently changed, until recently he had never paid any attention to girls, but his feelings on this matter had changed and he didn't know why???

The girl shyly introduced herself, her name was Macy...

After that meeting Macy and Glenn were inseparable when Glenn would visit the farm...

Both Macy and Glenn were natural introverts but they liked being together...

Neither one revealed much about themselves, but that didn't matter, neither one minded this unspoken agreement...

Macy watches for Glenn every day that summer but she knew he couldn't visit every day, he had revealed to her that his Uncle had custody of him, but since his Uncle had always been a bachelor, so his Uncle was always looking to relatives to help babysit...

Most of the time the two explored around the creek, but sometimes they would venture the length of the creek till I met up with the river...

One day as they were heading to the river Glenn noticed an old cemetery close to the creek.

It was very overgrown but Glenn wanted to investigate this new found place, he urged Macy to join him but to his utter surprise she would not join him, he looked around a bit then rejoined Macy by the creek...

Glenn didn't ask her why, but he figured she was just scared...

A few days later Glenn asked Macy if she had ever explored the old school.

To his shock Macy acted the same way as she did at the cemetery, but she did say that it was dangerous to be around that old building...

Glenn didn't push the subject any further. But Glenn had decided that on his next visit he was going to explore the old school, but he kept this to himself...

Glenn had never stayed overnight at the farm and one day he asked his relatives if he could come and spend the weekend, they agreed, and Glenn's Uncle was thrilled at the idea...

That Friday Glenn arrived for his weekend visit, but he did not seek out Macy like he usually did, instead he wanted to avoid her till he had a chance to explore the old school, he hadn't told her he was going to be staying the whole weekend that was a secret...

Glenn also had another secret he had saved up some money and had bought Macy a necklace...

That day Glenn entered the old school, the old desks were still there, books and journals...

On one desk carved into the desk he saw his great grandpa's name, as he looked around more he saw a carving that made his skin crawl at first, but he put off this notion as coincidence...

Later that day he caught up with Macy, at first he noticed she was crying, not knowing how to console her, he decided to give her the necklace, instantly her mood changed, she took the necklace, but her mood was very somber, then she whispered in Glenn's ear...

"I Saw You Enter The School. I Wish You Had Never Done That" then Macy turned and ran off...

Glenn was in shock. The rest of the weekend Glenn searched everywhere for Macy but he could not find her anywhere...

On Sunday he was walking back from the river when he noticed the old cemetery again, so he decided to explore it. At each grave he noticed names of people that must be relatives...

Springer's name was everywhere then he noticed a headstone that made his skin crawl something fierce, again he dispelled this notion as coincidence...

Later that night over dinner he decided to ask his relatives where Macy lived.

Macy had only once mentioned one time that she lived on a farm nearby, but she didn't say exactly where, but she said her father was super strict and it would not be a good idea for him to visit ever...

As Glenn asked about Macy, the relatives' faces grew very concerned. After Glenn spilled out his story, the relatives were in deep shock...

Finally one spoke...Son Macy lived here, but Macy died in a freak accident at the old school in 1860...

She was your great grandfather's younger sister...

Glenn couldn't believe his ears, his mind was racing...

Later that night while laying in bed he heard two soft whispers in a row...Glenn Please Don't Leave Me"...Glenn Please Don't Leave Me" as Glenn looked up he saw Macy in the corner of the room...

She was turned around so Glenn couldn't see her face, but he noticed she looked disfigured in a grotesque way...Then she started crying, then she disappeared...

Glenn was shell shocked and confused. When he woke up in the morning, as he was packing up his stuff, he noticed a carving in the old dresser he had never noticed before...Macy...

Over breakfast the relatives asked Glenn if he had slept well. Glenn didn't comment but the next words scared him so... That room you stayed in was Macy's Room...

As Glenn was getting in his Uncle's truck he looked up at the bedroom where he had stayed, and in the window was Macy the way he remembered her, and he noticed a glint from the necklace he had given her... Glenn never stayed here again...

Glenn has visited this place many times, the old school is gone but as he watches the woods he catches a glance...of Macy...then a glint...from the necklace ... Then he hears two whispers pleading...

"Glenn Please Don't Leave Me???

"Glenn Please Don't Leave Me???

Unfortunately he does each time...with tears in his eyes...

But he knows deep down...Macy will always be here...

THIS THOUGHT IS SAD...BUT COMFORTING AS WELL...

Something Has Watched From This Place...Something Never Human...Something Foul...Something Sinister...

GLENN HAS NEVER SAW THE SOMETHING...BUT THE SOMETHING HAS BEEN WAITING TO REVEAL ITSELF...

My First Paranormal

Hi everyone! So I had my first paranormal experiences when I was around 10 years old at my childhood house. At random times when I was in the kitchen, things would fall off the counters or I would hear knocks on the windows. We used to have those toy nets that we would hang our stuffed animals in. One night I and my sister were going to have a "movie night" where we put a projector in the net and shined it on the TV.

A porcelain doll happened to fall out of the net and right when It hit the floor someone or something knocked on the back window. We both looked at each other and ran out of the room and told my parents what happened. My dad got out the bat and went outside to see what it was but found nothing. My sister also had three imaginary friends that she would play with named Sally, Dee-da, and jukebox.

One night my sister said she saw a little girl with curly brown hair and a yellow flower dress in the mirror so I always wondered if that was Sally. Another time we were home alone and she came running into the room because she said she saw two people in the kitchen but when I checked nothing was there. I ended up playing music every night while I was going to sleep just so I didn't have to hear anything. One of the last experiences I had that I can remember was when we went over to play at our friend's house across the street. There were maybe five of us there and the family wasn't home. We decided to play hide and seek so I was the one counting.

They all hid but right before I hit zero, I heard this loud bang in the attic. All of a sudden my friend ran to the living room and said he heard someone knocking on the attic door as he was hiding in the closet that the door was in. We all got freaked out and ran back to my house. We told my parents what happened so they walked us back to check and we saw the blinds open like someone was peeking through. To this day I still have nightmares of that house and I also still have to listen to something before bed. Thank you for listening!

CHAPTER TWO

A glowing Orb

So this happened in early 2000... got up in the middle of the night thirsty
...walking into the kitchen to get something to drink. We had a fifty-
five gallon fish tank in the dining room... adjacent to the living room
area...next to my bedroom door... that we kept the light on at night... as
a night light for the house.... As I open my bedroom door and walk out
I see this glowing orb... In front of my fish tank slightly moving back and
forth... And my very large angelfish up against the glass swimming back
and forth like whatever it is playing with it...

Of course all this happened within a few seconds and whatever the orb
was... noticed me flew up into the vault of the room, did a couple loop
loops and disappeared... the only way I can describe what I saw is that
it looks like Tinkerbelle from the movies leaving this trail behind it...
So I really didn't think anything of it... thinking I was dreaming or half
asleep... a couple nights later sitting at the table with my two step sons
and happened to mention I saw the weirdest thing the other night in
front of the fish tank...

And before I could say anything else, my oldest step son said....was it
glowing... And that's when I knew I wasn't seeing things he saw too. I set
up a camera and never captured it again...

Still Confused

October 19, 2015 my husband passed away due to an infection that shut down his body and I thought that hospice would be my last resort. Unfortunately I had to put him in hospice. Now I believe hospice is just a legal way of killing people because all they did was put him on morphine and took away fluids and nutrients. After he passed I got him cremated and placed him in my safe so nothing happens to him. Due to family conflicts I never had a service for him. About six months after he passed I woke up and I always looked at my engagement ring, wedding ring and my two infinity bands. My engagement ring was loose on my finger and sometimes slipped off my finger so my wedding band was tight on my finger. I took both rings and switched them so I wouldn't lose my engagement ring. I woke up that morning, looked at them and went to run errands.

At the end of my errands my daughter and I stopped to eat at McDonald's as we were getting out of the car. Something made me look at my ring finger and my engagement ring wasn't there. In a panic we retraced our steps and didn't find it. I went home and told my mom about it. I was distraught so I went to lay down on my bed when I pulled the covers down there in the middle of the bed sat my engagement ring. Unbelievable right? Sometime after that I was in my room with my door closed and heard a very loud strong knock on my door. I said to come in but nobody did. I opened the door and nobody was there.

I went across the hallway to my mom's room and asked her if she knocked on the door. Now she needs a wheelchair to get around.

She was sitting on her bed and if she wants me she just calls me on the intercom. There was no way she could have gotten in her wheelchair, knocked on my door, wheel herself back to her room and gotten on her bed in that amount of time. My daughter lived in the apartment downstairs which has stairs leading directly upstairs. I thought it must have been her. I called downstairs and I could tell I woke her up. I asked her if she knocked. Of course I knew the answer would be no and it was. It happened once again but I left it when nobody was there again. A month after that I was with my mom helping her in her bedroom and we heard the kitchen cabinets open and slam shut. I went into the kitchen and nobody was there and all the cabinets were closed. The only other person would have been my daughter and she was at work. All this time I was getting my hair pulled on but it was gentle or I felt a breeze on my neck.

Two months later my mom was taken to the ER. My daughter and I were with her. She ended up having to stay overnight. As we were walking down the hall of the ER to leave I felt my ponytail being lifted straight up and it stood there. I did a side glance at my daughter and she said mom I see it too. We just kept walking like nothing was going on. I just happened to look over and noticed a nurse sitting there staring at me with her mouth open. As soon as we got to the doors to leave my ponytail went back to normal. We never really talked about it or told anybody what happened. My mom's house was foreclosed on forcing me to put her in a home and my daughter and I became homeless. We stayed in the car till we got into the YWCA. I ended up trying to kill myself but I was found and woke up in the hospital after a week then was taken to the mental hospital. After that I stayed with my friend and her parents for two years and then was asked to leave.

Anyway, from the day my husband passed, which I knew he passed before I got the call from the doctor, I dream about my husband almost every night and it's always different scenarios from him leaving me to live with another woman to being a loving couple. We were married for 24 years when he passed. I can't get rid of these dreams and they are so vivid and detailed that I have different emotions when I wake up depending on the dream. I still get my hair pulled gently and a breeze on my neck. I need help understanding all of this and what it means. If someone I know loses something I have to be in their house, close my eyes and something tells me what room it's in but not where in the room it is. I also get a horrible feeling in my gut that something horrible is going to happen to someone I know but I don't know when or who.

Unfortunately, it usually ends with a death or a car accident. I also, for example, know what someone is about to say even if we were just sitting in silence doing our own thing and then they say what I already thought they would. Am I crazy or is it something else? I would love any feedback. Oh, and just to note I was in the mental hospital for major depression disorder.

The Young Boy

Many years ago when I was just starting high school we lived at the edge of town so I had to ride the school bus every day. We had a few houses around us and three of those homes had children who also rode the bus. Our house was several doors down from them so I got off before the others. One afternoon when I got to our front door I discovered that it was locked. I couldn't find the house key hidden anywhere so I just sat on the porch to wait until my parents returned home. I figured they probably just went to the grocery store and would get back soon. I watched the school bus as it stopped to unload the neighbor's kids. Now, one family had several children ranging in age from about seven to about eighteen but I noticed only the youngest boy got off. He was the very last one off the bus and lagged behind the other neighborhood kids.
I thought it was odd and I figured that the rest of his brothers and sisters were probably sick and had stayed home. I watched him walk up the driveway to his house and thought that he was dressed rather nicely. Nice black slacks and a white dress shirt. Very snazzy! He rounded the little curve that led up to his house and I could no longer see him so I started in on my homework. After a while my parents pulled up and we went inside. During supper that night, I asked my mom where they went. She told me that the neighbors had come over asking for a ride to town to buy some clothes for the youngest son. Mom and dad didn't hesitate and

my mom purchased a nice set for him - black slacks and a white shirt. I just nodded and said, "Oh." Then all of a sudden I looked up at both of my parents and my dad noticed that I had gone white as a sheet (or so he said later on).

The first words out of my mouth were, "That's right. He passed away yesterday!!" Mom began to cry and nodded yes. I told them that I had watched him get off the bus that very afternoon!! They both just stared at me. I was in total shock. I told them that he was alone and that I had wondered where his other brothers and sisters were. I had completely forgotten that he had passed away a day earlier!

A couple of days later we attended his funeral. Yes, he was wearing black slacks and a white shirt!

This story is very true and if my parents were still alive, they would vouch for me. The boy looked like everyone else. He wasn't transparent or filmy and, no, he didn't float. He was just doing what he normally did - going home!

Few Ghost stories

So I have a few ghost stories, usually I don't like to tell them because not everyone is a believer but I figured here would be a good place to share a few memorable ones. My first encounter was when I was young when me and my brother were little sharing a room and I woke him up because I swore I seen something in our walk through closet after he woke up we realized it was a woman in a dress floating back n forth it lasted a few minutes until he turned the light on. Next was years later around nineteen when I lived with my ex and a lot of things happened in our apartment a subtle singing of a child late at night in the bathroom, my friends baby magically went from a crib to the other side of the room when it couldn'

I didn't have any other experiences really until I got with my fiancé in 2016 and I was in the bathroom mopping and I had an entire conversation with him from another room, seeing a shower walk through the hall not paying full attention thinking it's him.

Well about five minutes later his car pulls up and come to find out he wasn't even home so I have zero clues who I was speaking to. We moved about three years later and had a bit of activity in that house lights flickering back and forth a hole in the attic magically got patched up. I took pictures of the attic one night with a friend and in one picture a shadow of a woman is in the window. After we took the pictures we locked the door leading up to the attic and went downstairs about ten-twenty minutes later there was a thud and somehow the attic door screws all were pushed out and the door knob on the outside was on the floor.

I haven't had any actual ghost encounters in a while but living there I have nothing but night terrors. For three days straight I had dreams of being possessed or someone trying to possess me and woke up at 2:26 am on the dot. We bought a home two years ago and I now have

**nothing but vivid nightmares that I am almost half awake for as if I'm
in a dream but awake and can control them in a way.**

My Later Grandma

Growing up I was very close to my grandparents on my mom's side. I
was always at their house spending the night and going places with them.
My grandfather passed away in 1988 from cancer, and then my grandma
joined him in 2015.

Prior to my grandma's passing she moved in with my parents and my
mom took care of her before she had to go to a nursing home due to
getting sick. Moving forward, after my grandma was laid to rest, my
parents' house started getting a bit of activity. We would hear a low
voice calling us (sounding like my grandma), and footsteps, things being
rustled through like bags and drawers in the bedroom she stayed in,
which was also my room growing up. I moved back in after my divorce
in 2018, an occasional shadow of a tall man which we all believe is my
grandpa popped but in his younger age, and more recently a smaller one
that looks like my grandma. It's never been scary, a little comforting in a
way but I don't like going in at night without turning on the lights and
normally running through the house.

So into what happened to me today. I was having a bad day at work,
after I went to my parents' house to pick up my son, and found out some
news I was taken aback by. However I was looking through a box that my
ex-husband dropped off their house that was mine. In it I found a card
from my grandma and she signed it "love you grandma" well I showed
my mom, told her i want to get it tattooed and she said yeah good idea.
(I already have a memorial tattoo of an owl on my arm) then while we
were sitting there we heard something moving in the basement... to me
it sounded like the laundry room door then a few minutes later, there
was footsteps across the kitchen floor but it was tapping/clicking sound

like when her dog was walk in the kitchen when she heard the cheese wrapper, I was eating a cheese stick.

When I got home I showed the card to my boyfriend and was telling him about wanting to get the words tattooed either on my wrist or above my owl which is for her anyway. I went into the living room and was texting my mom about some things and my twenty two year old son about his wedding. All of a sudden I get a smell of cologne that lasts a few minutes, but it smells nothing like anything that my boyfriend has or my seventeen year old son who was sitting next to me. I brush it off and still texting my oldest and mom, it happens again but this time it smells like my grandma's perfume and it's right next to me.

I text mom telling her what just happened, as I'm typing, I get this cool feeling and the smell right in my face like in my nose .. I jumped up and ran in the room to tell my bf... He's like well you did bring the card back from your mom's and you were just talking about your grandma and the tattoo while holding the card. I went and finished texting my mom, said she's watching you and apparently she gave you a kiss to let you know everything will be okay and she's with me

I have had many experiences in this house.

CHAPTER THREE

Definitely My Grandfather

So a few things have happened recently mostly involving my little girl, her toys would go off when we go to bed. I would get up and turn them off and go back to bed, they would go off again, and I didn't dare go back into the living room until morning.

Other bits and bobs have happened to her, like she's pointing at the corner smiling and waving when nothing is there. We have heard noises in the house like someone moving about and banging, every night without a doubt I hear the same noise as if someone is walking and moving things up in the loft. Also bad things have happened. Well, one time it seemed she was pushed over when she was walking and most recently today she was in the back of the car when the door swung open while the car was moving.

I don't know if this is connected but definitely is grandpa after all the stuff that has happened. My granddad passed away five years ago and never got to meet my year old child. So I don't know if it would be him, but he would never try to harm her. I don't know what else this could be, it definitely scares me when I'm home alone cause I feel like I'm being watched.

A House In Wisconsin

I moved into a house in Wisconsin. Packing dishes away while husband was picking up more from the apartment. I heard someone stamp up the stairs. I went to look up stairs & found hangers in the closet banging against each other. No windows were open. I went back down & worked on the dishes, again someone stamped up the stairs. Then the lights went out. I went to the basement & turned them on. By then my husband came & I told him what happened. Then he heard someone go up the stairs & didn't see anything.

Then the lights went out again. We left with our belongings & told the landlord & he gave us back our money...like it's happened before! Since then we moved to VA. But every year go up & visit family & every year there is a for sale sign in front of that house. It's been 25 years now...I guess the spirit doesn't want anyone living there.

A Transplant Killer

Last night on Beyond Belief a woman had gone blind but her vision was restored through cornea surgery, she received someone else's cornea in both of her eyes. She went into a bar to grab a bite to eat; she was travelling and got a room at a local hotel. When she was eating she saw a man at the bar but she couldn't stop staring at him although her brain would tell her not to stare she couldn't help it. He got agitated and got in her face asking her problem was and she asked him if they knew each other and he told her they didn't but he still stayed in her face for a little bit longer.

When he walked away she decided to leave and go back to the hotel and get her things and leave but as she was going into her room he barged in behind her asking her who she was, asking her if she were the police and kept hounding her for information thinking she was some law enforcement although she wasn't. He pulled the telephone cord out of the telephone and tied her hands up then sat in the chair and drank until he passed out. She got off the bed, opened the door with her hands still tied behind her back and ran to the hotel office and had the man running it to call the police.

Next thing you know she's wrapped up in a blanket and the man running the hotel is giving her a cup of coffee while the police told her that she was very lucky and there was a warrant for the arrest of the man that tied her up for murder, he had killed the woman who she received the transplant from.

A column of white light

When I was 29, my beloved mother-in-law died of pancreatic cancer. It was swift and vicious – she was diagnosed on June 28th and was gone by August 5th. The night she died I was home alone with my newborn daughter. My other child was staying the night with my parents so I could get some rest. My husband was at the hospital with his brother; they were sitting with his mother. We knew the end was coming, but we didn't know how soon it would be.

As you might imagine, I was exhausted – being the parent of a brand-new baby, having a three-year-old, providing care for someone I loved who was dying – I went to bed around eight o'clock and went to sleep as soon as the baby drifted off. I don't remember what I dreamed at first, but I remember when the dream shifted. I went from some unremarkable dream circumstance to floating above a hospital bed. My husband and brother-in-law were there, talking in low voices.

I was looking down at my mother-in-law. Her face was slack; her skin had a yellowish-green cast brought on by the cancer's spread to her liver. Her eyes were closed, her breathing was ragged and slow. I hung there above her, watching her, knowing she was dying. I was dimly aware that my husband was administering morphine from the pump, and my brother-in-law was at the door, calling for the nurse. My eyes were fixed on her, and I could feel her energy rising from her body, rising toward me.

My breathing matched hers – shallow and slow, then slower, then gone.

I woke up a few minutes past midnight on the morning of August 5th when something tapped my forehead. I remember the relief of sucking in air and sitting straight up in bed. My daughter was in the bassinet by the bed, and I didn't have a pet in the house; I couldn't think what had touched me, but I could still feel it – almost like a two-finger tap right in the center of my forehead. I lived in the country then, and there were no streetlights nearby. My house was about a quarter of a mile from the nearest road, and there was a thick growth of trees that filtered any lights from passing cars, so I was surprised to see what looked like a column of white light in the corner of the room. Then I felt her presence in that light that seemed to grow, reaching toward me, falling across my daughter. The bassinet was full of light for just a moment. Then, the light was gone and the room was dark again.

Later that night, my husband came home. When I heard him unlock the door, I knew for sure that she had passed. He would never have left her otherwise. He didn't come into the bedroom because he didn't want to wake our daughter, but I went to him in the living room. He told me she was gone. She had died at four minutes past midnight, just at the moment when I woke up from that touch on my forehead, to see that column of white light in the corner of the bedroom. I believe with all my heart that she came to tell me goodbye, to see the baby one last time, and that through my dream that night I was with her when she died.

CHAPTER FOUR

Early Paranormal Discernment

I figured I'd go ahead and start with my very first paranormal experience. When I was 5 me, my parents, and my younger sister lived on the same property as my Dad's parents, in the house my Dad grew up in. My grandparents had wanted to give my parents more space, so they gave us this house and got a modular home. The entirety of the property measured 90-93 acres. With two ponds, and 4 homes at this point in time. From birth until I was 6 I was always with my grandpa. I even went on his mail route with him a couple times. He was truly my best friend. It was July 7, 1996 and we had just celebrated my little sister's birthday at what we called "The Big Pond". Everyone was there and we also set off fireworks to make it more fun. After it got to be late (8ish I'm assuming) everyone headed back up the hill to their homes.

As my Mom was tucking me into bed, she said I started bawling and begging to see Pawpaw Tommy. She reminded me that it was late, that I'd had a long day, and that I'd be exploring and playing with Pawpaw Tommy tomorrow. I refused to listen, and told her "I'll never see my Pawpaw again." It freaked her out, but she continued to console me and tried to get me to sleep. About five minutes later, the house phone rang. As she got up I told her "It's Nanny. Pawpaw is leaving to be with Jesus." Mom didn't say anything and rushed to the phone. I was right. My Pawpaw had had a heart attack, the ambulance was on its way, and he was completely unresponsive. My Nanny, Pawpaw Tommy's wife, was an RN, so we knew it was serious. Mom didn't say anything; she just called her parents to come get me and my younger sister so that my parents could be with my Dad's parents at the hospital. The ambulance came, and then my other grandparents came and took us to their house.

It was already strange that I had known that my Pawpaw Tommy was basically fighting for his life when the call came, but around 12ish (I remember seeing the numbers on the clock in my Mom's parents truck) I told my Maw Maw that "Pawpaw Tommy left us. He went to be with Jesus." Once again

I was told that it was all going to be okay and that I would see him soon. The next day my parents came and picked us up on their way home. My Sweet Pawpaw Tommy had passed sometime around midnight after doctors tried to get him stable. I didn't want to be around the funeral, and even refused to sit with the family graveside during his services. It hurt too much to lose my best friend at such a young age. This was pretty much the beginning of my experiences with the paranormal.

The Haunted Castle

As you know, the white lady is one of the most famous ghostly apparitions and exists almost everywhere in the world. I would like to tell you about our haunted castle. Around the 11th century a knight lived in a castle nearby, his wife was pregnant and the knight was happy that he would soon have an offspring.

The night of the birth came, but there had been serious problems. The knight's wife died without even seeing her child. When the knight saw that he had not had a son as expected, he became very angry. A few days after the birth, he brought the little girl to a family living on his land and gave them some money and orders to raise the child. In his anger, he joined the crusades and went to the holy land. After many years, he returned home with a guilty conscience.

His daughter had grown into a young woman, and he promised her to find her a rich husband. But, his daughter was already engaged to a miller's son. The girl broke off the engagement in her greed and was promised to a merchant 20 years older than her. The miller's son was devastated, on the night when he found out that she would not marry him; he cut his throat with a knife. A few weeks later, the wedding of the greedy bride took place. There was a big feast at the castle, and on her wedding night she died under mysterious circumstances. It is said that her timid fiancé took her that night.

Today she haunts the castle, and whoever spends the night in the woods around the fortress will meet her sooner or later. Then she asks if you know the way to the valley and for the right answer she offers you a coin but you should never take that coin or you are doomed to haunt the area with her.

Me And My Friend Jason

This story is about me and my friend Jason. A Little background story of both of us is that we have known each other since we were little kids about four years old. We pretty much did everything together like brothers. We messed around and into trouble a lot but somehow every word from Jason lets us go free with no troubles. I don't know how we were paired together by fate because we were always the opposite. He usually gets all the girls the best grades loved by everyone muscular, handsome, tall and whiter skin tone and especially Jason's family was rich. He was perfect; anyone would die and be reborn to be him. So on with the story we were 16 at the time, hanging out in the school parking lot. We were skipping school because there was a school assembly. You know, the whole school gathers for games and activities. We didn't like that so we were in Jason's car instead eating chips and drinking Pepsi. While we were eating we started talking about guys stuff.

Fishing, hunting and our future lives after high school. Somehow it went from our future college to girls. Example what we liked in certain girls that we would marry or date. And what pissed us off about them. Etc. Well because here in America hmon women marry White men and

Korean or Chinese looking celebrities from TV. But what Jason didn't know was that he did look like the handsome Korean guy. So then we finally made plans to go sleep over at his house. For the weekend for two nights because we had three days off of no school. So instead of his business Jason is lonely and what hmon say is Sheng Yu Ying like ah I'm so lonely and sad I wish I got someone to love me.

Only there was someone who could satisfy me. I'll take anyone, even ghosts. I yelled at him to shut up in Hmong.

I didn't even finish then all of a sudden someone threw huge pieces of dirt in our direction. Not hitting us but close. Since it's the fall and the woods it gets darker quicker. There was no one. I yelled out Neigh! You keep sheng like that someone throws dirt at us you better knock it off! Given how cocky Jason was he yelled out forget it even if there was a ghost it'll be better it came home with me. Then dirt is thrown at us but this time a deep rotten smell is there. And as well as a laugh like in the wind. We got scared and left school. We ended up going to his house early about 2:30 noon. We messed around again playing video games and watched rated r action films till 6:30 then we had dinner with his parents. Jason's family believed in technology and science while I believed in the spiritual Hmong stuff. And it was awkward to talk about it because they brought it up. Not a long time went by till 11 pm. And Jason's mom told us to go to sleep. I slept in Jason's room looking like a big hotel room apartment enough for a family of ten even his master bedroom to sleep in. But he only had another queen size bed aside just for me at the corner of the room. We went to sleep but not long someone opened the door like keeeeeeee.

Just enough to see someone not all the way. I couldn't see them because I slept at the corner which the door faced away from me. When it opened it was further away from the room than in the room. But Jason could because he was sleeping in the bed where it faced him. Did that a few times then the shadow ran away then the third time slammed the door. He woke up and checked who it was but no one. I slept in and didn't hear anything so he went back to sleep. Not long after 15 minutes some started scratching and knocking at the door gently. Jason thought his sister was messing with him so yelled out go sleep sis! Then it stopped and he went back to bed. Not even five minutes later the knocking became loud bangs like someone was mad at us trying to kill us and steal our stuff. This time I woke up. Jason got so mad he marched to the door and flung the door open while it was banging. No one. Then he spit and yelled in Hmong stupid Female dog why won't you go die where you're supposed to die and stop bothering is before he knock her teeth out.

Then he went back to his bed. He said it was probably his sister or worse ghost. Out of the blue we made a joke about elephant medicine, a Thai oil thing that makes girls like you but someone used super glue in his mouth in a movie. We laughed for a bit then went back to sleep. Whoever it was decided to visit us in spirit in our dreams. All I saw was a woman taking me walking in the woods. Now the one who took me was a ghost with long hair. She was scary looking, long tongue, long fingernails, and rotten skin all black and green. She had no eyes, just empty black eye sockets. And her voice had this echoing loud whisper that sounded like those people crying at the funerals. Oh dang it I'm even scared writing about this. Had this long torn white dirty dress? Every Time she walked there were bells in her feet that sounded ke klang ke klang every step. So anyways she told us to rest for a while. And she gave me something to eat: human eyes and worms. I screamed Ah mom in Hmong and threw it away.

I should've run but somehow I didn't. She got up and yelled at me for wasting food. And that she was going to take Jason soon but me first as his best man or Hmong people call it Meng Kong and find me a wife. Then she grabbed my arm and extended her long tongue for me to see. Told me to come with her and yelled a loud scream that almost made me deaf. Then I too got scared and jerked her hand violently and ran off.

I woke up instantly. I was sweating all over like I was at the Vietnam War. I was going to tell Jason when I heard something bizarre. He was singing like Hmong people talk like the word lu Xa. He was crying too. Like he finally met a past life wife or something. Like he was so sad like me gao sheng ehh ya. So I woke him up after 4 tries. He woke up and explained our dreams. He, on the other hand, had a beautiful girl in it. Someone is meeting him. Talking about all his sadness and loneliness. How she could make it stop. And that she was there to pick him up. They eventually made out and had of course slept with each other then he decided after to sing. Then I woke him up. I was so scared but, convinced me otherwise to go back to sleep. Because he has an amulet from my grandpa in his room to protect us. I finally did even though I was scared towards three am.

When I woke up his mom tried waking him up but failed. Then we noticed that he looked pale and almost dead.

Well it didn't take long till i woke up to find a horrifying scream from his mother. Jason's face was pale and cold almost like he was dead. He was rushed to the hospital. It didn't take long until the doctor came back to us in the waiting room. He gave the info that Jason was in a coma and may not wake up. I demanded an answer of the time of his conscious state. Yelling and yet this doctor was so calm like Jason's life didn't mean nothing. He gave me an answer maybe three weeks at least or better yet maybe more. Then he left. The mother wasn't much helping just sat there crying. I almost forgot to call my grandparents. Told them everything. My grandpa told me not to worry that he needed to perform the ritual. Tell me the fast way and slow way. The First one was to get Jason out of the hospital and into my grandpa's house and perform the ritual.

Basically the traditional Hmong/Chinese way. Or the slow would be I take something of Jason's and send them to my gramps and perform on his behalf. But it could take months. So I did the unthinkable. I devised a plan to sneak him out. I know stupid of me but I did it. I stocked the doctor and pickpocket his badge and snuck into the security rooms and logged onto the computer alongside the cameras. Temporarily. Tripped a wire and snuck Jason to his mom's car. Sorry no details how but I did it. So then we went to my gramps to perform the ritual. By passing my grandma scolding me. So anyways he began after thirty minutes of prepping. Thanking fully he was somewhat prepared. He performed. Halfway I can hear him arguing while singing and chanting. Tway tway let him go tway you dumb mother beeep blank. I was hitting the drum. Sounded crazy but I couldn't laugh. I lied a little. So anyways he kept going for a while then he spit out blood. Then came back down. Told me this ghost lady is too powerful. That he needed to send me instead since he's too old and weak. So he did an old method back from China that he was taught. He tied 2 long red strings with bells in the end around my risks.

Told me to come back when he rings it. And wrote spells with chicken blood and ink on my forehead. Then told me to sleep. He then burned a pot of incense which knocked me out. Thus took me to another world.

I entered another world. This world looked different from our own earth. It was dark and cold. It wasn't for the lights on the strings and bells on my risks I wouldn't be able to see. I began my journey and started walking searching for Jason into the wilderness.

During my journey I came across many spirits or dead ones in their own torment (very terrifying).

I'll give you example one spirit was hanging on the tree (suicide). 2 people being tied and beaten by a man reminding them of the affair. Another person being chained and burned then many creatures throwing spears at her. She screamed for help while I vaguely saw her sins unfold. I couldn't face anymore so I moved on, still shaking and covering my ears. I could've sworn I saw my dad walking by so I followed. I kept calling but he was one step ahead of me. It wasn't till he came to an area and stopped. He pointed in the direction of a road and disappeared. There in the road was the ghost and Jason. I ran and finally caught up. I had an argument with the ghost for a while till Jason told me to go back home because he found his wife. I said no ghost and humans can't be together and told the ghost she didn't let him go, don't be sad to me. She ended up forcing my hand and I ended up fighting her.

Oh I forgot to mention my grandpa did teach me the basics for ghost combat but only a few spells. During the fight the bells started ringing. I couldn't do much so I grabbed Jason's hand and ran towards the direction the string was pulling. She was chasing us even till the end where I went through the portal back to the human realm. Just before we went through it I heard my name called and turned behind me. Bad mistake (it might come back just to let you know). So we made it back and both I and Jason woke up while grandpa rang the bells. After that my grandpa remade a new amulet and gave it to Jason. Jason of course wasn't happy that I brought him back. I could care less. It didn't take very long till he finally forgave me and not long after things went back to normal. Six months went by and my grandpa passed and the mantle of Grandmaster was given to my older brother. But he ended up moving to California.

CHAPTER FIVE

The Former Owner

My sister moved into a home built in 1890. Beautiful big house. The second I walked in I felt crowded like someone was there. Not bad but there. My sister thought it was silly. When she moved out, her neighbor had a goodbye party for her. It was in the summer so it was light later. My sister took a cellphone picture of people eating and drinking. One of the "people" looked normal until above the knee. Below, there was nothing. When she moved out her friend, a nonbeliever was bringing boxes from the basement and felt a hand on her shoulder from behind. She turned around and saw a guy but the guy wasn't solid. He was transparent. My sister's friend said she never ran so fast in her life. I think a former owner wanted to stay with his home. He wasn't threatening, just there.

Her Colleague

I live in a small town called rugby, (where the game originated). It all started at rugby school many years ago, anyway I found out they do tours around the school which I have never entered because it's a private school. So a couple of weeks ago my husband and I went on a tour. The lady that took us round was telling us that a couple of weeks ago she was asked to go over to another part of the school to help a colleague with something. She popped over and on entering could hear footsteps upstairs.
Proceeded to go up , when she got there she couldn't see her colleague anywhere, deciding to go back downstairs, she turned her back and

suddenly she heard footsteps behind her running to the point she jumped back in fear and felt a 'rush of wind' go past her. But nobody was there, she ran down the stairs and as she shut the door heard the footsteps above and then got a text message saying her colleague was on her way.

My Twisted Encounter

I'm being honest and sincere. I encountered a situation one time where I witnessed a creature. It could have been a UFO, it could have been an alien, I do not know but what I do know is that they are real. I encountered the situation about two years ago and it took me by surprise. It was like stars truck the way I was drawn to this kind of energy and being a believer and seeing things that really exist that we humans don't think it's but they do. To make a long story short I encountered this situation with this alien type creature on a couple occasions. I noticed once I was chosen to see these days little spaceships started following me around like drones.... It doesn't matter where I went, what I did, what I was doing, who I was with, these little drones will follow me around and watch me.... They never harm me but they observe me as if they knew I saw something and were watching me to see if I was going to tell people. During some time I paid it no mind I deserved the situation of this fallen creature until it was left from inside of my house... When this creature was gone the drones left as well, thanks they quit following me and watching me in my life. I almost went back to normal for a little period of time that was two years ago...

But for now I can still sense and have the ability to know when something is out there which know that these identifying objects or creatures or other life beings are out there in the world among Us....... The scary thing that I think about is what if I would bring attention to what I saw.... As in letting somebody know that there was an alien in my house... Calling the FBI or police let them know that there's a creature in my house.., this strange falling mysterious thing I cannot explain what if they came and took it or before they arrived it would have killed me. I know what I saw I will never forget. People think I'm crazy but believe me it's not. I just wonder how my life would have been different if I were to show the world what I really discovered.....

San Diego Old Building

I worked in an old building in downtown San Diego. We originally were on the 3rd floor, but eventually moved to a bigger space on the 2nd floor. Nobody ever took the elevator, because it would stop between floors. It was kind of creepy. (Which may have just been because it was old, but it was creepy nonetheless) Shortly after we moved to the 2nd floor, weird things started happening. I was getting my desk together and placed a framed picture of my kids on my desk at the back of it.

I turned around to get some files out of the nearby file cabinet and when I turned back toward my desk, the picture I had placed at the back of the desk was now face down toward the front of the desk. I said something to my coworker who sat next to me and she said that she had just stirred her hot chocolate and left the spoon in the cup, turned around and when she turned back, the spoon was balanced across the top of the cup. Things like this happen on a pretty much daily basis. We had a large heavy safe in a locked room, along with confidential client info files on shelves that were bolted to the wall. One morning I came in and went to unlock the door to that room and had a hard time opening it, because something was blocking the door from the inside.

I got some help and when we finally got the door open, the room was in complete shambles. The top part of the shelves had been ripped from the wall and the rods holding the shelves were bent down to the ground. One of the shelves had been thrown out the window that had a strong steel mesh covering on the outside. The safe had been slightly pried open, but not all the way. It was a very secure room and there's no way anyone could have done this. We stayed in that office for quite a few years after that, but that seemed to be the climax of what was going on and not much happened after that. I

CHAPTER SIX

A Spirit Called Noah

Here's a ghost story of mine which I personally love because it validates my belief that spirits aren't always confined to one place and you can get random spirits hanging around you, and this is about a spirit called Noah. I haven't asked him how he happened to find me but I know it was probably around September last year because that's when activity in my house really started to increase. Like my mum would hear a really loud bang underneath her bed which had no explanation, my mum also heard a man screaming next to her and then near Halloween saw Noah right up close to her face and then around Christmas we had some photo frames moving on their own, one was on a wall which completely smashed and another was propped up on a shelf.

The little bit that I know about Noah is he did live in my town. He's in his 40's and he has a favorite area of the house he likes to chill out in but he LOVES attention and that's why he rarely ever spooks me out. Because I can sometimes tell when he's there and I'll wave at him so he knows I'm acknowledging him but my mum obviously never does that. I was doing a medium reading last week or so for someone who wanted to know if any spirits were around her and as I was doing it I felt Noah just go "wait I know her! Ask her about the phone piano, she'll get it!" So I did and it turns out this person had an app on her phone for a piano and it would play on its own and Noah told me he did that because he wanted to be her friend but it amazed me because I couldn't have known that, this was a random anonymous stranger online.

It confirmed for me even more that Noah was really there and he has told me before that the spirit of someone who technically died in my house is sometimes in the house with him together and I think he really likes those old tapes/cassettes because I asked him once if he wanted to listen to some music and he asked for a tape.

Spirits All Over

I have always been able to see/ feel spirits. I have a Lot of stories that have happened to me. But I start off with one that happened to me in college. After high school I didn't jump straight into college. I worked a 9-5 job doing tech support. I had a fiancé. And things were going pretty well at the time. I moved in with one of my best friends Kyle, we lived in an old apartment building.

There were spirits all over the place but they never caused any trouble; they would just hide in the corners of the hallways and stare as we all live our lives. But one day I found out my fiancé was cheating on me (I was sent the video evidence via phone) and I had a hard time with it. I went to work and when I got home our house was empty. There was a note on the wall that said check fridge. I went and looked at the fridge and there was a note taped to a beer. It said "I had my dad's construction company move us to my dad's house in Manhattan... your room is set up just how you had it here is the address see you soon." I hopped in my car and drove to my new "home" Kyle's dad built the house for him to live in but his new wife didn't want to live there so he rented it out to us.

It was a beautiful four story house. I took the entire 4th story as my domain. I had my own bathroom and five bedrooms to choose from and I used all of them. I slept really hard in this house. After being there a few months I started waking up at 3am. And I would see my door open and a white tall figure of must walk into my room.

It would come in and stand next to my bed, look around, then leave. And I could see it walk around the bannister and walk down the steps.it never creped me out. But I started thanking it. For looking out for us. One night I had a lady friend over and she usually never stayed after our... festivities but I wore her out and she stayed the night. And she wakes me up in the middle of the night and is speechless as the door was opened and a tall white mist was checking on us. I told her to go back to sleep. It's normal and it just is there to make sure we're safe. Then it nodded its head and left. This happened every night for the three years I lived in that house.

Back in 1998

Back in 1998,In the city of highland, san Bernardino calcific was staying in an apartment complex with my parents, my cousin Julian came to visit me. I just got out of Arizona boys ranch, in queen creek az... So I and my cousin Julian went out to the back car port in the alley to smoke a cigarette. While we were talking I heard a noise on the right side of me a little down the way.it was around 9:00 at night, I could hear something like something was in the trash can or and bushes. Then I told my cousin Julian do you hear that? He said yes I do...he heard the same thing I did. Well as I looked a little closer I noticed a small figure of a person. The figure we saw was a person the size of my hand opened. Really small. The best way to describe what we both saw was the gingerbread man... It moved into the middle of the alley way and stopped and started to stare at us... Then turned around and started running towards a chain fence, and I started to walk over to whatever it was to get a better look and when it ran it sounded slimly, the feet. And when it ran it ran from side to side, stiff...I made it to the fence and looked to see what it was in close range and it was gone...no where's in site... The figure we saw looked like something evil; demonic...ever since then I'd always see strange things all over that area...

My Strange Dreams

I have a really strange story about dreams I had from a young child to eighteen years old.

I still do not know what they meant or were trying to tell me. At the time, (of course I was young), I thought it meant that I was going to hell because I wasn't baptized(my grandma the "catholic" always told me that I will go to hell unless I got baptized!).

So, I was sleeping and then I started dreaming the I am a captive of these horrible looking beings, almost like zombies but more like human monsters, they are dragging me through these tunnels that had caves and in the caves were huge fire pits like there would be in Hell, they were throwing people in the fire, the sounds just echoed so loudly, the noise they would make and screaming and horrifying laughter, seemed like they just kept dragging me along farther and farther into the tunnels. Then I would wake up.

The other dream was that I was on a pier that was over the ocean and just walking along by me in the dark and I see this place that looked like a restaurant or a house, no signs anywhere, no numbers on the building, it was the only building on this pier that I never saw an ending to.

I walk inside and it does look sort of like an abandoned old house. I turn to the left to look down a hall, and then look to the right and right in front of me is this seven foot tall man with no head. I tried to scream and run, but he grabbed me, put me over his shoulder, then dropped me head first into the umbrella stand/container thing, and I am screaming and flailing around trying to get out.

I heard footsteps walking down the hall so I decided to be real still and quiet until they faded away. I finally was able to knock the container over and run, but now there were just these long hallways, some had windows that all I could see was the ocean and no pier. All of a sudden, something grabbed me from behind as I was running, and I was able to tell that it was the tall man with no head, I kept screaming and trying to break loose from his tight grip, he had me over his shoulder again, all of a sudden he grabbed me with both hands and through me through the window!

All I remember next is hitting the glass, then I woke up all sweaty and I couldn't breathe, my heart pounding out of my chest. I would army crawl on the floor from my room to my parent's room.

As I am crawling I get to their doorway and look up, I see a shadow man walking in front of my parents' bedroom window, now I feel like I am just going to die right there, I hurry and run to my Mom's side of the bed (my Dad would really get pissed if we went in their room at night) and hide under the overhang of the water bed right next to the night stand. I knew that's where my Mom kept her gun. This time I was going to be prepared if something tried to grab me. Then I would be woken up by my Mom in the morning telling me to go back to my bedroom.

Now I had these same dreams until I was about eighteen years old, but in the dreams I was still that young girl of about 6 or 7 years old. Yah!!! So can anyone tell me what it could have meant or try to tell me? Am I doomed to go to Hell?

CHAPTER SEVEN

My Night Shift

I am a police officer in a small northern Indiana town. I work third shift and I am the only officer in town. My closest backup can be anywhere from 5 to twenty minutes away. The town I work for is an old farming community. It's full of old houses, a real old graveyard etc. One night while I was out on patrol, the dispatch center had gotten a call about 2 possible intruders inside this really old religious building in the next town.

The building once served as a sanatorium then later a cult had purchased and then left. Because of the size of the building I was requested by the Sheriff's department to assist them with clearing the building. By this time it is about 2 AM and the owner who arrived told us he believed the intruders left. I and 4 other officers made entry into the building. After clearing the first 2 floors we concluded that nobody was inside at least no humans were inside beside us. We decided to go up the 3rd floor and check the attic to verify no vandalism had occurred.

Mind you there is no power in this building and we are clearing it with flashlights or our gun mounted lights. I was the last officer to the third floor. At the stairwell door, I took a 2x4 and wedged the door open. We walked down the dark hallway still announcing "police ". I then hear a thud behind me and I look back and the door I propped open had shut. The 2x4 was missing. We got to the attic access and all of us heard a male moaning from the attic. We all ran up the stairs with our weapons drawn thinking the possible intruders were in the attic hiding but when we got up there we found nobody. We concluded that the only people inside were us. We all exited the building and I remember the Deputy radioed to our dispatch advising we were going back in service and that the building didn't need police there but a priest.

Stalked

What would you do if a family member came to you claiming their house was possessed by something evil? My dad had a family member living with him for a few years that was into playing with Ouija boards. This person was not a devil worshipper but also wasn't religious. He might have just been doing it as a form of entertainment or a way to test if the Ouija board could really work. My dad and this family member began to fight a lot which led to them really disliking each other.

Once this person moved out of his home, he started experiencing some paranormal stuff such as waking up in the morning with a lot of unexplained scratches up and down his legs and arms. My daughter's toys that he has there for her to play with when we visit turn on in the middle of the night. He started having intense health issues in the last few months, as well as a series of bad luck with finances, relationships and just feeling exhausted with everything in life. Because he is a born again Christian he believes that whatever this could be could be there to test his faith. I hate to say it, some days it seems to be working as he is starting to question why it's taking place and why he wouldn't be protected by not only the paranormal but the series of bad luck he seems to be facing recently.

Some people also believe that when turmoil is in a home, it's an invitation for evil to enter. I do believe in the paranormal but I also believe in some situations there are other explanations, such as this could be....some type of bugs causing the scratches, batteries from the toys could be going bad, sometimes people just hit bad luck in life and of course he is getting into the older stages of life and this could seem worse than it is in his mind. Either way, as his daughter and closest confidant, I'd appreciate some advice please.

A Woman In Purple Robe

My husband and I bought our 1st home in Cincinnati in 1991. A couple weeks after moving in, we were making our bed and bickering over that was doing a better job with the fitted sheet. We started hearing what sounded like pacing in our attic. The longer we bickered, the faster the pacing got. I guess it finally dawned on us because we stopped and stared at each other.

The pacing got slower and slower then stopped. We were both like WTH was that!? We thought maybe it was windy and wires or tree branches were banging against the house. We went outside. Barely a breeze. Checked the whole house inside, including the attic. Nothing. We went back to making the bed and we decided to pretend to still bicker. The pacing started again and got faster and faster the longer we continued.

My husband would have friends over to play poker sometimes. More than once, while some were ribbing each other, they would hear the pacing.

There was a day when a friend came to visit and brought a friend. We had a stray cat we adopted as kittens. They were a few weeks from being weaned and my friend wanted to pick out one.

The three of us had gone to the living room to talk. Earlier I had made the comment that my husband was out. My friend's friend leaned forward and was looking down our hallway. She said "If it's just the three of us, who is the woman that just walked into your guest bedroom?" I of course got up and looked everywhere. I asked if she could describe her. This woman looked at me like I was nuking futz. She said she was wearing a long purple robe and had a salt and pepper bouffant hairdo. When I said, "Well, I've personally never seen her but you see, our house is haunted ", this woman jumped up, said to my friend "I'll wait for you in the car!", and ran out the door. I'm pretty confident she laid eyes on the individual that would pace when anyone argued in our home

The Black Figure

So around 2 or 3 months ago, I was in bed it was around 2:30 AM and I was lying there trying to sleep, when I heard something or, someone, whisper in my ear "wake up" I felt breath in my ear, I shot up from my drowsy state but, no one was there.....

I felt a shiver run down my spine, I led back down, and tried to forget about it, but then just as I was falling asleep, it happened again only this time the voice said "help me" I once again shot up from my sleepy state, and once again, no one and nothing.....

I choked it up as my mind was playing tricks on me being that I was half asleep, but later at around 4:00AM I was awoken by something tapping me on the back... I sat up, rubbed my eyes, and realized, no one was there....

I went back to sleep trying to ignore it, but then I felt something trying to pull me and I mean literally PULL me off my bed, I shot up and screamed..... but then I realized nobody was there.... it was now 7:30 "ugh, time for school" I thought to myself....

Later, after school I got home from school, had dinner, did some homework, played some mine craft, and got ready for bed at around 9:30, later at around 3:00 in the morning, I heard the voice in my ear again, this time it said "never leave, always here" I sat up, rubbed my eyes again and saw no one was there....

Then I heard footsteps outside my bedroom door, my heart started racing, "m-mum?" I said trembling, no answer, and then I saw something that will haunt me forever. I saw a black figure in the corner of my room that had red eyes. I just sat there in fear....

I quickly dove under my covers, I'm not sure how long it was before I fell back to sleep, when I woke up the next morning, the figure was gone, and everything was as it should be...

It's been a few months since then and nothing has happened to me since.....

I don't know who or what that figure was or what it wanted, I just pray that it never returns....

CHAPTER EIGHT

Love Struck Ghost

When Brad Culp was a student at Miami University in Oxford, Ohio, there was a rumor that the town was one of the most haunted places in America. When Culp started an on-campus magazine, he couldn't wait to write about several of the area's most famous phantoms. Not long after his story published, though, he kept finding himself thinking about one ghost in particular—the ghost of Oxford Milford Road.

As the story goes, many decades ago, probably sometime in the 1940s, there was a young man courting a young woman in a rural part of town. Because the woman's parents didn't approve of the match, each night he visited under the cover of darkness. After her parents went to bed, the young woman would sneak out of her farmhouse and flash the lights of her parent's car three times. Then her young suitor would ride his motorcycle down the road.

"One night he took the turn right before her house a little too sharp," says Culp. The motorcycle went one way, he went the other. His injuries were so severe that he did not survive. Rumor has it, however, that his loves truck ghost still haunts this stretch of Milford Road.

Curious, Culp, his girlfriend (now his wife), and a friend decided to head out there one night to see if they could verify the tale. His girlfriend was worried she'd be completely freaked out. "She believes more in that stuff than I do," Culp says. But he was mostly concerned that his suspicions—that none of this was actually true—would be confirmed. On this particular night, as Culp passed the abandoned farm, an idea came to him, and he pitched it to his girlfriend (how could she not say yes?). Though reluctant, she relented, and Culp turned a short way into the farmhouse driveway.

He killed the engine and flashed his lights three times. "No joke, there was a single headlight that appeared three-quarters of a mile down the road," Culp says. "You saw it start to come, going pretty slow. It kept coming and coming. My wife was freaking out. It was coming closer and closer."

As a collision seemed imminent, Culp turned on his car's lights. He expected to see a kid on a bike, bailing out from his prank now that he'd been caught. "But there's nothing there. The light is just gone," he says.

They got out of the car. They walked around, trying to figure out what it was they could have seen. "To this day, we still talk about it. I saw something I cannot explain," he says. If you get him and his wife around a campfire, they'll swear up and down that the story is true. And if you're ever in Oxford, Ohio, consider parking for just a few minutes on Oxford Milford Road at night to test your own nerve.

The Ghost of La Parva Ski Resort

Throughout Latin America, you'll hear variations of the story of La Llorona, or the wailing woman. Sometimes she's lost her husband. Sometimes she's lost her children. Sometimes it's both. But in La Parva, a ski spot in the Chilean Andes, the wailing woman is named Lola, and everyone in the area swears they knew her before she died. "A local restaurant owner said he dated her," pro skier Drew Tabke says, adding that the ski patroller he heard the story from pointed at the exact hut where this tale takes place.

The story starts on a nice day in peak ski season. Lola and her young son planned to spend the day on the slopes. "As can happen in the Andes, a thick fog rose up from the valley, which often precedes the arrival of a real storm. The clouds enveloped the two as they were making their way down from the top of the mountain, and they lost contact with one another," Tabke says.

Desperate to find her son, Lola began screaming his name as she ran through the thick fog. Unable to see clearly, though, she stumbled down a steep slope and began sliding toward a rocky couloir.

"By chance, a local lift operator who was returning to his cabin came across her body. He was afraid she was dead, but on closer inspection, he found she was still alive, just barely," Tabke says. Her body was covered in lacerations from sharp rocks, and the only word she said—in the faintest whisper—was her son's name.

The lift operator worked to carefully pull her body to his cabin, which was just up the hill. He bandaged her cuts as best he could and then ran to fetch the doctor. Together the doctor and lift operator made their way back to his hut, the fog hanging thickly in the air. When they arrived, though, the bed was empty. Just the bloody sheets remained.

"Neither the woman nor her son were ever found," Tabke says. But locals report hearing her wails for her child whenever they're near that lift operator's cabin.

And here's the thing: Tabke does not believe in ghosts. Something, however, changes when he arrives in Chile each winter. Maybe it's the fact that, from La Parva, you can see up to Cerro el Plomo, an Incan child-sacrifice site. Maybe it's because Tabke has simply read so many magical realism books by authors like Juan Rulfo and Gabriel García Márquez. But sitting alone in his cabin in the Andes, with the wind whipping and the candles flickering, he swears that every now and then he just can't tell if what he's hearing is a woman or the wind.

The Crying Lady in The Dakota

When The Dakota was built, it was something of a modern marvel. According to Curbed New York, an 1885 Real Estate Record and

Builder's Guide regarded it as "one of the noblest apartment houses of the world." And since its opening, it has housed many famous residents, including Peter Tchaikovsky, Lauren Bacall, Rosemary Clooney, Connie Chung, and Maury Povich. But The Dakota made a new name for itself after John Lennon and Yoko Ono moved into the building in 1973. Why? Because Lennon claimed he saw a "crying lady ghost" roaming the halls, and after Lennon died—directly in front of The Dakota—Ono said she witnessed Lennon's ghost sitting at his piano.

The Jersey Devil

While this one is not a "ghost" story, the tale of the Jersey Devil has withstood the test of time—and for good reason. Stories of the winged beast are truly terrifying. But who or what is the Jersey Devil? According to Weird NJ, the infamous creature haunting the Pine Barrens is the child of Mother Leeds, a Pines resident who conceived her thirteenth child in 1735. At the time, Leeds had no idea how she could care for (let alone afford) another kid and so, in exasperation, she raised her hands to the heavens and proclaimed "Let this one be a devil!" Leeds got her wish. Moments after birth, her healthy baby boy grew horns and claws and bat-like wings. Legend has it the "devil" then killed his mother before attacking onlookers.

Phantom Steamboat on the Tombigbee River

In February 1858, a steamboat named Eliza Battle set out on a cruise down Alabama's Tombigbee River. Onboard were 60 passengers and more than 1200 bales of cotton. But when the cotton caught fire on March 1, guests and crew were overcome by smoke and flames. 33 perished on (or in) the Tombigbee. It is said those ill-fated passengers haunt the river to this very day, and on brisk nights, people have claimed became known as the Bell witch. Of course, no one knows her true identity, but legend has it she's the ghost of a former neighbor, Kate

Batts. It is also believed the witch played a role in the untimely loss of John Bell, who died from poisoning.

The Ghost of Henry Dixon

Tunnel ton may be a small, unincorporated town in rural Indiana, but it is big in the ghost hunting community. Why? Because Tunnel ton is home to the Tunnel ton Tunnel—a.k.a. The Big Tunnel—where it is said numerous ghosts still linger, both on and beneath the grounds. However, the most famous tenant is Henry Dixon, a night watchman whose body was found just inside the tunnel in 1908. Dixon's murder was never solved, and many have reported seeing the watchman on patrol—lantern in hand. Locals have also been "chased" by Dixon.

The Legend of the Hamburger Man

While the origins of Hamburger Man are unclear, the reason for his moniker is obvious. Urban legend says the half man, half monster kidnaps his victims, drags them deep into the woods of Sand Hills State Park in Hutchinson, Kansas, and— once there—grinds his victims into hamburger meat.

Devil's Den

In the summer of 1863, hundreds of thousands of soldiers descended on Gettysburg, Pennsylvania, and many lost their life. According to How Stuff Works, more than 50,000 infantry men were left dead, wounded, or missing, and rumor has it some of these soldiers still haunt the battlefields, particularly Devil's Den: a rocky enclave where 1,800 died. One woman claims she felt a hand grab her ankle at the historic site, and several others have seen

CHAPTER NINE

Last sight of a departed friend

Returning to my flat in Westminster one afternoon, I saw two friends coming towards me on the other side of the street. I had no time to stop and hoped they would not notice me. I crossed the street behind them and hurried home.

At breakfast time, a friend rang to tell me that the man I had seen the day before had died in the night. I was amazed and described how I had seen him and his wife apparently in perfect health. My friend exclaimed that that was an impossibility, as he had been ill for some days. The widow, I may mention, is still alive.

The disappearing woman

This occurred more than 10 years ago, but is still vivid in my mind.

One afternoon, my attention was arrested by a woman moving through the throng on whose face was a most dreadful expression of distress. So appalling was her grief, with great tears rolling down her cheeks, that I had an unconquerable impulse to follow her.

I could not see her again. I looked all about, followed in the way she was going, trying to see again my vague impression of black, clinging garments, a tall figure, grey, disordered hair and that face of trouble. She was nowhere.

I turned to my companions, who were amazed at my outburst. They had seen nothing, but, at the time, we were passing the Bloody Assizes.

Holiday haunting

House was modest, possessing one of the most charming small gardens I ever saw.

Ghosts soon declared themselves. The manifestations were pronounced and various. My sisters were visited in the night by a figure walking in their room and, when it came between their beds, they fled shrieking.

A figure passed the housemaids in the corridor, cold hands were laid on hands lying outside the counterpane, bells rang without being pulled.

The village priest came with book and holy water, the spirits were effectually laid and we slept in peace.

Now I have read, in Mrs Stirling's The Diaries of Dummer (1934), an account of similar manifestations at the same house in 1851. The old house has been pulled down, but I hope its garden still shelters the poor houseless shades that wander by night.

The lost village

In Scotland last year while walking through an ancient forest with my husband, we took a shortcut through the wild glen and intended to walk down the bank of the Fillen to Crianlarich. We came to an open space, flat and treeless and full of sun-haze.

As we entered, my husband remarked: 'I don't like this place, it's too old and dead.' I was about to reply that I felt it only peaceful, but I suddenly had the sensation of depression almost amounting to hopelessness.

What I 'saw' was more a feeling as if all about me was snow, under a leaden sky, and behind me there were people and their eyes were without hope.

My husband saw that I was oddly frightened and so we left for Crianlarich. We told them at the hotel that we'd felt spooky at one place in the forest. The late Mr Alistair Stewart said: 'Oh yes, that would be where a whole village was lost in the snow and they all starved to death.' We are both Celtic, but neither of us is in the least psychic. One thing I do know is that even if I were chased by Hitler and his grizzly gang, I would not enter that forest again.

Don't miss out!

Visit the website below and you can sign up to receive emails whenever Paul Kuipa publishes a new book. There's no charge and no obligation.

https://books2read.com/r/B-A-FHPQ-EEFXB

BOOKS 2 READ

Connecting independent readers to independent writers.

Also by Paul Kuipa

About the Author

Paul Kuipa is one of the best upcoming Aurthors. Born in October in the year 1993, at Dangamvura in Mutare. Which is the second biggest city in Zimbabwe. He grew up in Nyanga in Chinhenga, one of the rural areas. Thats where he finished his primary grade and moved to Harare, the capital city. After his secondary level, he then moved to South Africa, Johannesburg to further his studies. And started his writting career at Unisa College. From there he is unstopped, publishing book after book.